The Full Bhoona

Amy Glasgow

Best wishes

Ringwood Publishing

Glasgow

First published in Great Britain in 2017 by
Ringwood Publishing
www.ringwoodpublishing.com

e-mail: mail@ringwoodpublishing.com

ISBN 978-1-901514-38-4

British Library Cataloguing-in Publication Data
A catalogue record for this book is available from the British Library

Printed and bound in Scotland
by Scottish Print

Contents

Foreword

My grandfather Qadir Baqash came to Glasgow from the Punjab in 1956. My father Ghalum Rasul Tahir joined him in 1960. In 1964 together they opened what is now officially recognised as Glasgow's oldest Indian Restaurant, The Koh-I-Noor.

This book, *The Full Bhoona*, in the preparation of which I have been fully involved, is the story of my family, and the contribution our restaurant has made to Glasgow life and Glasgow culture over the past 50-plus years, a contribution it continues to make under my stewardship, having picked up the baton from my father in 2010.

It is a proud story this book tells. The story of my family, who created and sustained a wonderful restaurant, and the story of the many other families that have come to love and cherish it as a treasured Glasgow institution. I am proud that many of these regular customers have contributed their memories of the restaurant to this book.

As well as being the story of my family, our restaurant and its many customers, I wanted this book also to be the story of traditional Punjabi food, simply made and superbly presented. I hope that this book will encourage you to recreate your favourite Koh-I-Noor dishes in your own homes just by following the simple recipes outlined in this book, the ones that my grandmother used to create the signature 'Koh-I-Noor' style. I also hope of course that while doing that you continue to return regularly to the restaurant!

I thank Amy Glasgow very much for writing this book with the guidance of my helping hand, and Ringwood Publishing for enabling the story to become established in print, but most of all I want to dedicate this book to my family who created and sustained the restaurant and the wider family of friends and supporters whose loyal custom has made it the cherished Glasgow institution it has become.

May you all enjoy the story and continue to enjoy the food that is its central core.

—Waseem Tahir

Introduction

The phrase 'the full bhoona' has many connotations across Scotland, developed over the years to mean giving it everything, putting in as much as possible, so you wouldn't be too surprised if you overheard a Glaswegian calling out with pride: 'Ah gie'd it the full bhoona, by the way!'

It's a fitting interpretation, given that the origin of the phrase stems from a dish that appeared on the first menu of the Koh-I-Noor, a restaurant that was opened due to the hard work and determination of one family—you could say they gave it everything, they gave it 'the full bhoona.'

When they put a dish on the menu called the 'Full Bhoona'—a large lamb bhoona served with a sizeable side salad—it's unlikely they knew then how famous that saying would become. Now the oldest curry house in Glasgow, the Koh-I-Noor is over fifty years old. It has been a labour of love for the Tahir family, bringing traditional Indian and Punjabi cuisine to the hearts—and stomachs—of Glasgow, Scotland, and beyond.

The much-loved restaurant situated on North Street today is very different from where it all began. The humble beginnings of this renowned curry house stretch back to 1956, when current owner Waseem Tahir's grandfather, Qadir Baqash, came to Glasgow from Pakistan. In 1960, Qadir was joined by his son Ghalum Rasul Tahir and in 1964 they opened the Koh-I-Noor restaurant in Gibson Street with only six tables.

Since then, the family has endured several trials and successes to build the curry house Glaswegians know and love today. Over the past five decades it has become a favourite with locals, restaurant critics and celebrities alike.

—THE— KOH·I·NOOR RESTAURANT

THE RESTAURANT

en the Koh-i-Noor first opened in 1964, it was the first Indian restaurant in Gibson Street. In response to its growing popularity, an extension was added in 1974. It continues to be run as a family business- by the present owner, Rasul (or Russell) and his son Waseem, the grandson of the founder.

The family hails from the Punjab and Punjabi specialities such as Paratha and Bhuna Lamb are particularly recommended. The Koh-i-Noor Restaurant prides itself in the fact that the excellence of the food is matched by the courtesy and efficiency of the service, and by the spotlessness of the kitchens.

The restaurant is favoured by many well-known people, from show-business, politics and the media. Its reputation goes far beyond Glasgow and the itinerary of numerous distinguished visitors to the city would not be complete without a visit to the Koh-i-Noor. It has been commended by Egon Ronay for many years, and Christopher Drew Smith the Good Food Guide.

The management and staff welcome you to the restaurant-whether as a regular patron or as a first-time experimenter in the delights of Indian food.

Due to extensive water damage in March 1982 the Gibson Street building had to be demolished, and a new site found for the Koh-i-Noor.

In November 1983 the new Koh-i-Noor was opened at 235 North Street, Charing Cross, in more spacious and luxurious style, incorporating the comfortable lounge bar and the Berkeley Function Suite as additional features. The management guarantee the same high standards on which their reputation was founded, and on an even wider selection of food and wines than before.

THE DIAMOND

e most famous of all diamonds, the Koh-i-Noor, was found at Golconda in India towards the end of the 13th century. Originally, it weighed 186 carats. This immense stone was held by the Mogul emperors and later by the Indian princes.

In 1849, the Koh-i-Noor was presented to Queen Victoria. It was re-cut to 106 carats and since then has featured prominently in Britain's Crown Jewels. The Koh-i-Noor was included when a new crown was made for Queen Elizabeth, the Queen Mother - it can be easily recognised in the cross that occupies the front of the crown.

Meaning literally, 'Mountain of Light', the Koh-i-Noor is traditionally supposed to bring good luck to a woman who wears it

TEL: 0141-221-1555, 0141-204-1444

History

1960s

1970s

1980s

6

1990s

2000s

2010s

Tahir Family Tree

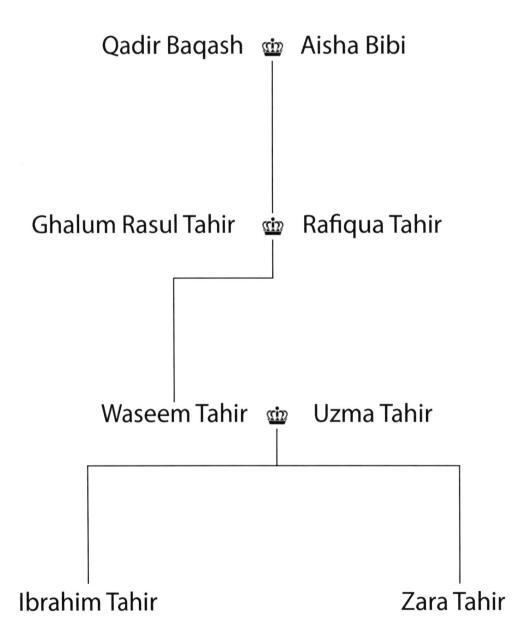

Qadir Baqash ⚜ Aisha Bibi

Ghalum Rasul Tahir ⚜ Rafiqua Tahir

Waseem Tahir ⚜ Uzma Tahir

Ibrahim Tahir

Zara Tahir

Timeline of the Koh-I-Noor

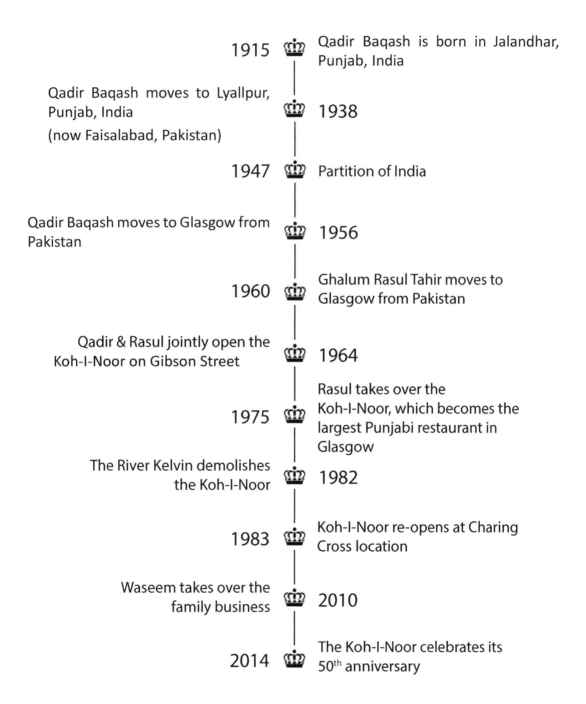

1915 — Qadir Baqash is born in Jalandhar, Punjab, India

Qadir Baqash moves to Lyallpur, Punjab, India
(now Faisalabad, Pakistan) — 1938

1947 — Partition of India

Qadir Baqash moves to Glasgow from Pakistan — 1956

1960 — Ghalum Rasul Tahir moves to Glasgow from Pakistan

Qadir & Rasul jointly open the Koh-I-Noor on Gibson Street — 1964

1975 — Rasul takes over the Koh-I-Noor, which becomes the largest Punjabi restaurant in Glasgow

The River Kelvin demolishes the Koh-I-Noor — 1982

1983 — Koh-I-Noor re-opens at Charing Cross location

Waseem takes over the family business — 2010

2014 — The Koh-I-Noor celebrates its 50th anniversary

The Diamond

At the end of the 13th century, the massive Koh-i-Noor diamond was unearthed at Golconda in India. It weighed an impressive 186 carats, and was the pride of the Mogul emperors and Indian princes alike, before being seized by the British and sent as a gift to Queen Victoria in 1849. The diamond was recut to 106 carats, and since then has featured prominently in the British Crown Jewels. The Koh-i-Noor was included in the new crown made for Queen Elizabeth, the Queen Mother, and can be easily recognised in the cross that occupies the front of the crown.

Meaning literally 'Mountain of Light,' the Koh-i-Noor is traditionally supposed to bring good luck to the woman who wears it, and holds a special place in Indian mythology. For the past half-century however, Koh-I-Noor has been the name of one of the longest-standing Indian restaurants in Glasgow. It, like the diamond that came before it, epitomises the very best that the endlessly varied sub-continent has to offer. It is a fitting name for one of the oldest-surviving Indian restaurants in Glasgow, carrying its own legacy that is now over 50 years old, and so often referred to by its customers as 'a wee gem.'

Aisha Bibi with her son, Rasul, and his eldest daughter in the late 60s

Early History

The Tahir family originated from the district of Toba Tek Singh, which is named after a religious Sikh figure, Tek Singh. Legend has it that Tek Singh was a kindhearted man who served water and provided shelter to worn out travellers passing by a small pond, or 'toba' in Punjabi. The pond eventually took on the name Toba Tek Singh, and the city and entire district followed suit.

Located in central Punjab, Toba Tek Singh is made up of large areas of lowlands, and Qadir Baqash and Aisha Bibi were inhabitants of a village that was called 'Chak 50/wb' or simply, 'number 50.' '/wb' relates to the branch of the district the village is in, in this case, the west branch. In the 1950s, this village was mostly agricultural, with little money or future to be built, but even there, food played an important role. Their main diet was made from the ingredients they harvested: spinach and corn. Most days that meant saag, a spinach curry, and makki di roti, a cornflour patty or flatbread. They would also have lassi, a yoghurt milk drink packed with protein to keep the men going as they worked tirelessly in the 45°C heat, hand-ploughing the farmland. In the mid-1950s, Qadir and Aisha decided to move to the United Kingdom, where they found a home in Glasgow's Gorbals.

Located on the south bank of the River Clyde, the Gorbals has long had a reputation as a gritty and rough area of Glasgow, as well as being a heavily industrialised area—a far cry from a rural village in Pakistan. But in 1956, this is where Waseem's family began their journey, which was the same time that the redevelopment of the Gorbals began.

In 1957, a Comprehensive Development area was created, and over the next two decades, street after street of traditional Glasgow tenement housing was demolished to make way for sub-standard prefabricated deck blocks and other forms of inferior social housing, most of which has also been flattened to make way for the 'New Gorbals.' Despite the problems it faced, the Gorbals was also famed for its community spirit which could not be crushed—despite the often adverse circumstances its residents faced.

Qadir Baqash and Rasul Tahir: the family business is born

The First Steps

In 1960, Qadir Baqash had saved up enough money working as a door to door salesman to buy himself an ice cream van, and it was in this year that his son, Ghalum Rasul Tahir (nicknamed 'Russel' or 'Rusty') came to Glasgow and found work as a bus driver. He worked extra shifts every hour he could, each week putting away pennies in savings, and in 1963, he purchased a shop on Gibson Street in the West End. In June of the following year, his father bought the space next door, which they combined to create their first restaurant in 1964.

Their decision to open a restaurant was the result of the passion that Qadir and his wife, Aisha Bibi, had for food. As a housewife, Aisha spent much of her time cooking traditional meals for the family, which she loved doing. She always said the way to a man's heart was through his stomach. One day, Qadir decided to try to help his wife in the kitchen and got a real buzz from it. He loved being involved in the cooking as well as the eating, so for six months, prior to opening the restaurant, he spent much of his time cooking with his wife, learning the traditional methods and recipes. The way to a Glaswegian's heart, too, was through their stomach.

Later on that same year in 1964, the Shish Mahal restaurant—now located on Park Road—opened directly opposite in Gibson Street. Two other curry houses, Shalimar, and Himalaya opened nearby in the early 1970s, and the street soon became known as the 'Glasgow Curry Mile.' The owners of the Shish Mahal are first cousins of the Tahir family, so the street was very much dominated by this large extended family.

When the Koh-I-Noor first opened its doors in 1964, with only six tables, its format was somewhat revolutionary, and it began a long crusade to give Indian and Punjabi cuisine the reputation it deserved. For Glaswegians, largely unfamiliar with real, traditional Indian food, it was certainly a wonder to behold.

For the first two years after opening, Qadir and Aisha worked tirelessly in the kitchen, recreating, and serving dishes from their Punjabi home, while Rasul worked front of house. The restaurant became famous for their special, the 'Full Bhoona'—a large dish of bhoona lamb with a special salad. A traditional dish, the word 'bhoona' is South Indian and translates as 'brown and thick' which is exactly the consistency of a great lamb bhoona, with a rich gravy.

By 1974, they had refurbished the restaurant from 50 to 100 seats, with 55 members of staff and regular queues out the door for every lunch and dinner service. In those early days, the menu was small, simple, and traditional. There were only chapatis, or parathas, with tandoors only making their way into the Glasgow curry scene in the 1980s. Basic curries like chicken bhoona, curried mince and vegetables, lamb curry and biryani dominated the menu. Back then, there was no such thing as a 'takeaway,' so they soon had customers bringing all sorts of containers, pots and pans with them to the restaurant, over-ordering curry, and taking it home with them. To this day, they still have customers who come from England, Wales, and Northern Scotland, bringing large, empty pots with them, and ordering curry to take home and freeze—so fond are their memories of this revolutionary curry house.

With the restaurant booming, Rasul used the money to buy his father some land in Mareed Wala—the next village along from where the family originated—bringing with him the first car, first tractor, both being the first heavy machinery the village had ever seen. Qadir Baqash returned to a quiet, rural life and a comfortable lifestyle, while his son Rasul took full control of the restaurant business back in Glasgow in 1975.

Saira Bibi of the Shish Mahal fixing her older sister Aisha Bibi of the Koh-I-Noor's hair for a photo in 1968 on the banks of the River Kelvin

Ghalum Rasul Tahir as a young man

Expansion

Between 1979 and 2000 the business continued to expand. In 1970, Rasul's younger brother, Abdul Ghuffar, came to Glasgow, and it wasn't long until he too joined the family business, despite originally training as an accountant.

In 1979 Rasul made the decision to expand with his brother Abdul into the manufacturing business, making and selling curries to wholesale businesses and supermarkets. It became so successful that in 1980 they bought a church in Kilbirnie Street and converted it into their distribution centre for this ever-expanding enterprise of Maharani Curries, Scotland's first trademark wholesale ready-to-eat curry manufacturer, which was created by the Tahir family. The company, under the management of Rasul and Abdul, supplied curry to Farmfoods, Co-op, and all the Greater Glasgow hospitals, with a new curry each week. This was the only business of its kind anywhere in Scotland, finding a new niche in the market. The company and the factory were sold in 1985 after 6 strong years of trading, as the two brothers were keen to focus on the Koh-I-Noor brand, which were always at the heart of their business.

In 1985, the Koh-I-Noor opened in Coatbridge, followed by another restaurant in Airdrie in 1987, which ran successfully under Abdul's management. Later on in 1996 the Paisley branch of their restaurant opened. Before the turn of the millennium, the second, third, and fourth branches were opened; but after the year 2000, all of the restaurants were sold to concentrate on the Charing Cross restaurant.

Opening the Koh-I-Noor at Charing Cross

The boss at the office in the 80s

Rasul enjoying one of his favourite pasttimes

Another of Rasul's pasttimes: coaching the Koh-I-Noor football team in the 70s

Interior of the Charing Cross location, 1980s

A Step Back

Back in 1982, the business took a massive hit as Glasgow City Council claimed that the building on Gibson Street had suffered irreparable damage from the River Kelvin, and the family were given three hours' notice to evacuate the building before it was demolished. The entire block, from the restaurant to the flats above, which, at this stage, the family owned a not-small percentage of, all had to be quickly evacuated to prepare for the demolition. Their restaurant disappeared in moments, their livelihood gone, and quick decisions had to be made as to where to go next.

Rasul made the bold decision to open a takeaway next door and bought over the Himalaya so that they could continue trading and meeting customer demands, and they quickly re-established a reputation with customers for providing delicious, authentic food and quality service. In 1983 they moved to their current location at Charing Cross, the space originally home to the Berkeley, an upscale and sophisticated space that could accommodate a large number and suited the needs of the business. In the early 1990s they refurbished, and have continued to adapt the style and layout of the restaurant to create the current look, which, on entering the restaurant, provides you with a very authentic and traditional atmosphere, with bright colours, elaborate patterns and tasteful décor.

Over the course of fifty years, the family went from running one restaurant to four, as well as a wholesale curry business, showing not only the growing demand for Indian and Punjabi cuisine, but also how much the hard work of this small family had paid off. Strangely though, by the end of this four-decade span, the business had returned to running just one restaurant, deciding that at times, less is more. Rasul decided to shift the focus of the business back to their crown jewel, the Koh-I-Noor restaurant at Charing Cross, and it has continued to thrive ever since.

Rasul overseeing construction after disaster struck the Koh-I-Noor in 1995

Disaster strikes again

In 1995, disaster once again struck the Koh-I-Noor restaurant. In an echo of the 1982 catastrophe, the Koh-I-Noor restaurant was forced to close once again. A huge chimney block from a derelict building next door crashed into the restaurant. Fortunately no diners were present at the time or lives would have been lost. The family and staff were forced to immediately evacuate the building.

As a result of the incident, water started to pour into the restaurant causing considerable damage. Ordeal by water for a second time. It was supposed to last only a few months but turned out eventually to be over a year, because of a legal wrangle with Glasgow City Council which the Koh-I-Noor eventually won.

After such a long time closed, Rasul decided that the front Lounge Bar needed a major facelift and along with that new toilets were added into the front of the restaurant, so all told it was a major process of refurbishment that took place.

Refurbishment before disaster strikes again

Refurbishment pictures of restaurant post disaster in the late 90s

The Third Generation

From the 70s through to the early 90s, Waseem and his family lived in one big house consisting of his father Rasul's family, and his Uncle Abdul's—four adults and twelve children under one roof. Waseem has many fond memories of big family birthday parties, where his mother, Rafiqua, and aunt would cook for the family. His favourite dishes, oddly enough, are the same traditional meals that his grandparents would have eaten back in Pakistan: saag curry and makki di roti. At least once a week, Rafiqua would make this traditional meal for them, despite the fact that a traditional saag takes at least five or six hours to make from fresh spinach leaves, spinach puree and spices. To save herself time, Rafiqua would make large portions and freeze them so she didn't have to spend hours in front of the stove each time her son wanted her delicious saag curry.

Growing up in Glasgow, the family also ate a lot of European food— including homemade fish and chips very week. Waseem's cousin Nadeem, from the Shish Mahal, used to come to the house and say to Rafiqua, 'Aunty, can I get fish and chips!' The culture that they grew up in meant that they didn't eat curry every night, trying to take in the western food of Scotland, which made it even more special when they sat around to enjoy a curry. They feasted on chicken curry, or chicken shorba, which had a thinner gravy that was almost soup-like, and was served with potato or cauliflower. They ate simple curries with simple ingredients, like chicken and potato, spinach and cauliflower, lamb and brussel sprouts. None of the curries had names at this stage. The names like tikka masala, pasanda, even korma, that we now use to identify curries are simply a westernisation of Punjabi cuisine, but in Waseem's home growing up, it was simply lamb, chicken, or spinach.

In 1989, at the young age of 14, Waseem followed in his father's footsteps and the third generation of the Tahir family began working at the restaurant after school. He started off in the kitchen cutting onions, a job he quickly grew to hate. He worked tirelessly from six p.m. to one a.m. on a Friday, and 12 p.m. to one a.m. on a Saturday, using the safety goggles from the keg room to protect his eyes from the bothersome onions. It was a job that seemed to go on forever, no thanks to the cooks in the kitchen, Waseem recalls: 'As soon as the other staff saw me wearing the goggles, they'd just send me another bag of onions!'

After three months, he was promoted to dishwasher, where he worked with four other staff members, furiously washing and drying to keep up with the ravenous customers in the dining room. Six months later he learnt to make chapatis like his grandparents before him, until eventually he was placed front of house, greeting customers and taking their coats. He was so careful to be polite and gracious to customers, he frequently made £10 to £20 in tips in a single night.

Today, Waseem continues to manage and run the restaurant at Charing Cross. He continues to uphold the family values of hard work, friendly service, and great food. Waseem says he would love to open a small restaurant that focussed on the more traditional way of cooking, serving just a small number of dishes based on the simpler, back-to-basics style curries with only a few ingredients. But for now, his family's legacy continues in the form of the famous Koh-I-Noor at Charing Cross.

The father and son double act ready for another publicity picture after major refurbishment in early 90s

Aisha Bibi and Uncle Abdul feed Waseem his first (but certainly not last) samosa

*Waseem as an eight-year-old on the opening
night of the Koh-I-Noor at Charing Cross*

Taking the company car out for a spin

Waseem dining with Billy Connolly in the 80s

The Scottish Parliament
Pàrlamaid na h-Alba

<u>Motion S4M-10345:</u> Sandra White, Glasgow Kelvin, Scottish National Party

<u>Date Lodged:</u> 16/06/2014

<u>Koh-I-Noor Celebrates 50 Years with Charity Week Fundraiser</u>

That the Parliament congratulates the Koh-I-Noor Indian restaurant in Glasgow on celebrating 50 years serving the people of Glasgow, making it the oldest curry house in Glasgow; applauds the decision by the owner, Waseem Tahir, to hold a fundraising week for Scottish charities, which will benefit Stroke Scotland, Marie Curie, Beatson Cancer Charity, Yorkhill Children's Charity and Alzheimer's Scotland, and looks forward to Koh-I-Noor's continued success in Glasgow.

Kind regards,

Sandra White MSP

50th Anniversary

In 2014, the Koh-I-Noor celebrated a very special event: its 50th anniversary. To mark this momentous occasion, Waseem and the restaurant team used it as an opportunity to not only celebrate, but also to raise money for local charities.

For a week in June, customers could purchase a ticket for £20 which included a meal and live entertainment, and the money raised was split across five different charities: Stroke Scotland, Marie Curie, Beatson Cancer Charity, Yorkhill Children's Charity and Alzheimer Scotland. Across the week, they managed to raise an incredible £5,000.

Waseem said: 'We wanted to give something back to the city to mark our anniversary and what better way to do that than helping those Glaswegians in need. The charities we worked with are ones who carry out a great service in Glasgow and beyond.'

The charitable efforts from both the Koh-I-Noor team and its customers is a true testament to the loyalty and love its customers have, and the warm and giving nature of the Tahir family.

Still going strong at 50, the Big Yin's favourite curry house

Dining down the decades: Billy Connolly, right, at the Koh-I-Noor in the 1970s with Resul Tahir in the 1980s, above, and in the 2000s, left. Inset, the original Koh-I-Noor in Gibson Street

Let's TIKKA walk down memory lane

by Jay Williams

I T is the curry house to the stars, the place where Hollywood A-listers go when they're in town. But Glasgow's Koh-I-Noor has one celebrity fan who has been there almost from the start – comedian Billy Connolly.

The Big Yin, 71, first visited the restaurant in 1967 and has been a regular ever since.

Owner Waseem Tahir, 30, whose grandfather opened the doors in 1964, said Billy has been one of our loyal supporters over the years. He's said it's like a home from home for him. He's always in good spirits when he comes in, joking with staff and customers. He even pops into the kitchen to talk to the chefs.

'Back in the day when he was a regular customer he always used to have lamb bhuna, but nowadays he has vegetarian dishes like saag aloo and vegetable samosas.'

The Koh-I-Noor was one of the first restaurants in Glasgow's Curry Mile on

Star: Waseem Tahir and Alan Cumming

Gibson Street in the 1960s, along with the Shish Mahal. They are the city's oldest existing curry houses.

Waseem's grandfather Qadir Bayash, grandmother Aisha and father Resul Tahir, now 74, worked tirelessly to build the restaurant's reputation.

Now situated in the city's Charing Cross, the Koh-I-Noor remains popular with celebrities, including rock bands Wet Wet Wet and Deacon Blue. Other star diners include Scarlett Johansson, Keanu Reeves, Lulu, Alan Cumming and cricket legend Imran Khan.

Mr Tahir Jnr said: 'Billy has been great to us over the years. My father had a stroke a couple of years ago and Billy was asking for him. He last came to see us in January, and he was in fine form, as always.'

A series of charity events is planned for next month to celebrate the restaurant's 50th anniversary.

Celebrity: Resul Tahir with singer Lulu in the 1980s

KOH-1-NOOR 50TH ANNIVERSARY
CHARITY WEEK 16-20 JUNE 2014

MON16TH   STROKE ASSOCIATION
TUES 17TH   MARIE CURIE CANCER CARE
WED 18TH   BEATSON CANCER CHARITY
THURS 19TH   YORKHILL CHILDREN'S HOSP.
FRI 20TH   ALZHEIMER SCOTLAND

GRAND FINALE 27TH JUNE
Auctioning memorabilia from
50 years of Koh-I-Noor history

6PM TILL LATE £20 ENTRY
includes meal and live entertainment

The fourth generation: Ibrahim (above) and Zara (below)
learning from the best, their father Waseem

The Next Generation

Continuing the legacy that their great-grandfather began over half a century ago are Zara and Ibrahim Tahir: the fourth generation to run the family business. While Zara and Ibrahim are still learning the tricks of the trade, Waseem has instilled in them the qualities of service that make the Koh-I-Noor so special to all who dine there. Passed on from generation to generation are the values of hard work, hospitality, and the family's passion for food.

Rasul and Ibrahim testing recipes at the Koh-I-Noor

Rafiqua and Rasul with Zara and Ibrahim

Rasul on grandfather duty, with Zara

Ibrahim's first solo trip to the restaurant

Fish and chips at the Koh-I-Noor

Zara approves of the new chairs at the Koh-I-Noor

Rasul's grandchildren Ibrahim and Zara learning to cook at their grandfather's village house

Memories

Before: buffet-style, 80s

Buffet present

Curry Makes Glasgow

Ask any Glaswegian, and most of them will tell you that Scotland's favourite takeaway is a curry. Scottish people have adopted and fallen in love with the flavours of India, and the Koh-I-Noor has had a large part to play in this love affair.

As one of the oldest Indian restaurants in Glasgow, the restaurant delighted locals with a completely different dining experience. Its first menu held only a handful of curries, each one lovingly prepared using traditional ingredients and methods. The curries that we know and love today are varied and complex, and are, to an extent, a westernised version of their predecessor. But the Koh-I-Noor continues to bring the city of Glasgow traditional homemade curry in a relaxed setting.

In the sixties when the Koh-I-Noor first opened its doors, it was the first Indian restaurant on Gibson Street. The same year, the Shish Mahal opened up and later on in the 1970s, two more curry houses followed suit. The stretch became known as the 'Curry Mile'. The most notable of these restaurants still remaining is the Shish Mahal, to whom the Tahir family are closely related, and despite whispers, they have supported each other for generations. These two families built and began the curry legacy in Glasgow.

Dining out in Glasgow and Scotland has grown and changed significantly over the years. This is due not only to the introduction of Indian cuisine, but also to the style of eating that the Koh-I-Noor pioneered. The Koh-I-Noor was the first restaurant to bring a buffet-style option to the Glasgow curry scene, providing an indulgent way of dining with incredible value for money.

Today, there are over twenty curry houses in the city centre of Glasgow, all taking inspiration and influence from the Koh-I-Noor, which led the way for Indian and Punjabi cuisine. Even with fifty years behind it, if you were to look up the best Indian in Glasgow, the Koh-I-Noor appears on most lists, considered a Glasgow institution by many. You don't know Indian— Glasgow style—until you know the delights of the Koh-I-Noor.

A Cultural Icon

There is, obviously, a reason celebrities and locals continue to flock to the Koh-I-Noor. It is for all intents and purposes an institution and a part of Glasgow's food history. The Koh-I-Noor has heavily influenced Glasgow's culinary culture, and in doing so, gained customers for life. It is a testament to the success of the restaurant and its long-standing influence on Glasgow's curry scene that customers still come from all over Scotland and England, arms full of Tupperware so they can take home an entire freezer's worth of curry from their favourite curry house.

Billy Connolly has been a regular visitor for over five decades and continues to pop in for his favourite dish, saag aloo, and many people refer to the Koh-I-Noor simply as 'Billy Connolly's favourite curry house.' Over the years, Waseem and his family have played host to many Scottish and international celebrities, from Lulu to Derren Brown and Alan Cumming, to name a few.

In the following pages, you'll find a collection of memories from the Koh-I-Noor. From celebrity photos to stories from the dining room, these memories from the past are a testament to the incredible influence that the Koh-I-Noor has always had on Glasgow culture, and continues to have today.

The Koh-I-Noor's Wall of Fame

'India's Hell's Angels' —The Sunday Times

Memories from the Dining Room

After more than four decades at its current location, the Koh-I-Noor has had some colourful visitors over the years. As well as developing a regular and unwavering customer base, the restaurant has played host to some of Scotland's most-loved celebrities, from Billy Connolly to Alan Cumming, as well as internationally recognisable faces, from Guns N' Roses to Derren Brown.

Despite these A-list customers walking through the door, the restaurant never forgets its everyday customers that continue to return year after year, showing loyalty and a real love for both the food and the service of the Koh-I-Noor. Loyal customers return to enjoy not only the food, but the company and the unique and traditional style. Since it first opened its doors over fifty years ago, the Koh-I-Noor has been bringing the people of Glasgow authentic Punjabi and Indian cuisine, something that had, until then, been somewhat alien to the people of Scotland.

The fact that the Koh-I-Noor's customers are so happy to share their fondness for the food, the atmosphere, and the family behind the restaurant shows what an effect it has on the people who visit. These are their stories.

'Still can't believe it was 2010—more than a decade into my career as a restaurant reviewer—before I wrote an article about the legendary Koh-I-Noor.

Particularly as, during that period, I'd probably popped in for a curry on at least a hundred different occasions!

A few years earlier, in June 2005, the Glasgow curryhouse was actually the venue for the second-half of my stag night. Some guys prefer a bit of debauchery Amsterdam-style (I took my wife there last year and got charged corkage) but I settled for a wee night at Shawfield Greyhounds.

Which actually seemed quite appropriate, of course, as my life was about to go to the dogs…

Anyway, after losing a fortune - great training, I suppose, for life as a married man - I escaped the clutches of the bookies and directed my pals to the Koh-I-Noor.

They knew exactly where it was, of course. The Koh-I-Noor seems to have been in business for about 200 years (how on earth can it only be 50?) and the restaurant that shares its name with a famous diamond is an absolute gem.

I was initially attracted to the Charing Cross restaurant thanks to the amazing buffet. It was the first restaurant in Scotland to offer an all-you-can-eat feast and, on my first visit, I think the waiters had to put down speed bumps…

In fact, I only slowed down thanks to the gurgling fountain at the centre of the buffet. Yep, it's always a struggle to fill your plate without having to rush to the loo…

My favourite dishes at the Koh-I-Noor? Well, it's hard to look past the properly-marinated chicken tikka and the succulent tandoori lamb chops.

And, even as a man who's well-known for his love of a paratha, no trip to the Koh-I-Noor is complete without a well-fired onion kulcha.

Mmm… think I'll pop round for one right now.

Here's to the next 50 years!'

—Tam Cowan
Journalist, The Scottish Sun

'No visit to Glasgow is complete without a stop at the Koh-I-Noor! I love going there with my family or a bunch of friends because the place just feels like you're having a delicious dinner in someone's home. It's a truly Glasgow experience!'

–Alan Cumming

Actor'

Fabulous food and famous all over Glasgow as the gastronomic Indian gourmet's first port of call. Always felt a wee bit special when the spicy aromas pointed my feet towards the front door and into the ocular feast that precluded the aural treat I knew was waiting. A palace for palates.'

—Tony Roper,
Actor, comedian, playwright

'I was only six days into my "roving reporter" role with STV Glasgow, the new channel set up in June 2014 to cover the goings-on in Scotland's biggest city. The Commonwealth Games and the Scottish independence referendum were both on the horizon, but we needed to find some strong, local names and events to keep us busy over the opening weeks of the programme. I was brand new to television, and was very much still finding my feet.

Enter the Koh-I-Noor.

I knew of the restaurant and I'd walked past it hundreds of times over the years of living in Glasgow, but—much to my shame—I'd never been in. One of my colleagues suggested we film a "behind the scenes" video package in the venue, due to its history and claim to being the oldest Indian in the city, which I thought was a great idea for a colourful TV package.

We got in touch, and it just so happened that the restaurant was celebrating 50 years in business by holding a week-long charity fundraiser. The timing was perfect.

Myself and my cameraman for the day Marco Federici headed along just before lunchtime. Marco—an Italian well-versed in culinary delights—was eager to sample some of the Koh-I-Noor's renowned dishes. I, on the other hand, was nervous about portraying the restaurant in the right tone. A half-century anniversary is a pretty big deal, particularly if it's your job to adequately tell that story in a three-minute television report.

But then we met the restaurant's owner Waseem Tahir, and within minutes he'd put me at ease. It was just a "wee" charity fundraiser, he told me. We'd go into the kitchen and have some fun with the filming, he said.

Waseem was brilliant. I'd recommend you give the video a watch if you can find it: it's buried in the depths of YouTube, but you'll see how good Waseem is on camera. He was a natural.

He took us through how they made some of the restaurant's signature dishes, and within half an hour Marco had got enough mouth-watering shots to make any viewer drool. I'd got some great answers from Waseem, and I'd done my all-important piece to camera in the restaurant. The food looked—and smelt—wonderful. It tasted even better.

It turned out the restaurant was fundraising for five consecutive nights for five separate charities, and they were also auctioning a bunch of Koh-I-Noor memorabilia to raise even more funds. I thought it was a fantastic gesture, and I was delighted that STV Glasgow were able to cover it considering the Koh-I-Noor's ties to the city.

I've been back to the restaurant a number of times since our day of filming there in 2014. I filmed around 150 packages during my tenure with STV Glasgow, but the one at the Koh-I-Noor really stands out for me. A few occasions I've returned with work colleagues—some with my former employers—and others with friends or family. It has an atmosphere which, I think, is very hard to find elsewhere in Glasgow. The Koh-I-Noor is almost like the city's best-kept secret.'

—Colin Stone
Broadcast Journalist and Senior Reporter, Radio Clyde News

'Forty years after we graduated in geology at Glasgow University, we got together for what turned out to be a fabulous reunion! We selected the Koh-I-Noor as the venue because we used to frequent the first restaurant in Gibson Street and many of us had our graduation dinner there all those years ago. Indeed, most of us first experienced the delights of a curry for the first time at the Koh-I-Noor. Some even took their wife there for that first date!

For this reason, it was very nostalgic for us, and we were delighted that the quality had not changed. Still fabulous Indian food after all these years.

Of the 16 who graduated, 12 managed to join us and there are already plans to bring us all together again, travelling from around the globe.

The Koh-I-Noor has a special place in our lives from those great years at Glasgow University.

Our visit was pure nostalgia and a delight as always!'

 —David Mason
  Loyal Customer

'Throughout my undergraduate days Gibson Street was the place to go. The Koh-I-Noor, the Maharajah, the Green Gate, the Shish Mahal. An exotic aroma hung over the whole place, from the bridge over the Kelvin up to Bank Street.

At first the choice was limited. Lamb curry four shillings, lamb and mushroom $^4/_6$, chicken curry five shillings, chicken and mushroom $^5/_6$ (ask a senior citizen to convert). On a student grant (remember those?) I usually went for lamb. If you brought along your own pan you could get a carry-out, which was cheaper.

Later when we lived in Montague Street the Koh-I-Noor, just round the corner, became our Saturday lunchtime place of choice. Nothing like a curry brunch, overlooking the Kelvin flowing below, to kickstart the weekend. Even after our first child was born we kept up the ritual, bringing in the baby buggy to sit beside our table.

So it was a disaster when one morning after a night of heavy rain we awoke to find the whole shebang had been washed into the Kelvin. And that, we thought, was the end of that.

Not so. Like a phoenix the Koh-I-Noor arose again, on a huge new site on North Street. Rooms within rooms, with dinky wee chairs, all beaded and belled. Friendly staff and interesting pictures.

And the Koh-I-Noor has never looked back. We still enjoy our Saturday brunches there, and our children come too when they're about town.'

—Mary McCabe
Author of Everwinding Times, Stirring the Dust and newly released Two Closes and a Referendum

'I first started going to the Koh-I-Noor in 1975 at the age of 18. I was introduced to curries by my work mates at Ever Ready Batteries, where I worked as a van salesman; then, the Koh-I-Noor was based in Gibson Street.

I have continued over the years to use the Koh-I-Noor on a regular basis for business and personal occassions and have found the quality of the food to be of high standard throughout the years.

I still use the Koh-I-Noor today even though I travel 20 miles to get there from where I live near Falkirk.

I would like to thank the owners and staff of the restaurant for their pleasant manner and continued quality of food.'

> —Jeffrey Forrest
> *Owner of House Blinds Ltd.*

'My first encounter with the Koh-I-Noor restaurant was in 1982. It didn't take long for me to become friends with the owner, Mr. Tahir, and get to know his son Waseem. Since then, my family and I have enjoyed countless delicious meals at the Koh-I-Noor, and I would certainly recommend the restaurant to my friends.'

> —Mian Sadiq
> *Loyal customer*

'I've been a customer of the Koh-I-Noor for 35 years believe it or not! I was in my mid-20s when I first went. Primarily I went with my company on a Friday night or a Christmas night out. For about 10 years we'd take between 35 and 85 people to buffet night—every year the numbers seemed to grow.

One year, on a Christmas night out (and of course, I'm the organiser for all of this—collecting all the money and so on) there were some new guys who I didn't really know that well. They went and stole all of the silver signs above the meals on the buffet. Of course, Waseem's up to high dole asking "where have all my signs went?" and I've not even started on my main yet. So I tracked them down to the Bon Accord—a pub about 300 yards away where they'd stashed them—not to steal them as such but just for fun. I was raging. I had to run to the Bon Accord to pick up all of these curry signs, but Waseem was relieved when I got them all back.

I went in a huff that night—I almost didn't go back to the restaurant! Waseem would have been down a bunch of signs and a paycheck. But eventually I went back and paid the full bill. We've been good customers for years and we know Waseem really well, he even sometimes lets us stay on later, sometimes until 2 or 2:30 a.m. even after the restaurant has officially closed.'

—Sandy Sutherland
Loyal Customer

'I have been eating in the present Koh-I-Noor since it opened in North Street, so I've been a customer for—I can't even tell you how long. Three generations of my family have eaten at the Koh-I-Noor, and Waseem was only a little boy when I first started going—he used to wear his dinner suit and bow tie running around the restaurant. It was his father who was in charge when I started going with my family. However, now Waseem's at the helm and I'm sure we've spotted one or two celebrities. One time, we even saw Allan Cumming with his family, and Waseem tried to get me to go up and get his autograph, but there was no chance—I'm not that kind of person.

I had young children and eating out for dinner can be expensive, so it was only once the kids grew up that my wife and I started going to the Koh-I-Noor every second or third Saturday, until she passed away eight years ago. However, I still go, and 95% of the time it's on a Saturday.'

—Ian Watson
Loyal customer

'Curries from the Koh-I-Noor are remembered in a nostalgic haze of expectation, wandering through the autumnal chill of Gibson Street in the 1960s. Entering through the door into the Koh-I-Noor was to pass into, not just another world of sights and smells, but another continent. The velvet wallpaper, Indian artwork, the unusual quarter-modes of a unique music culture and those spices added to the feelings of expectation and wonder. For a boy who had rarely been out of the East End of Glasgow, and the only "Koh" he had encountered was the "Co" in "Co-op," this was a completely different world.

The waiters bridged two cultures with their Indian sub-continent appearance, juxtapositioned, unexpectedly, with razor sharp humour delivered with Glaswegian accents and vernacular "Jeezo, you'll be turnin' intae wan, if ye order any mer o' they pakora pal."

I am reminded of the waiter who responded to my wife's concerned question regarding the sloppy curry stains that covered my side of the white tablecloth. "How do you manage to get them so clean?" she asked. In his impeccable Glasgow accent he answered, "Nae problem hen, we just throw in an extra dod o' Fairy Liquid and the fairies lick the stains aff!"

In those days, if you were a vegetarian, as I was, this was the only place where you could sample a decent meal that was not a damp salad or a rubbery omelet. The favourite was always vegetable pakora, followed by cauliflower, potato and pea curry with fried rice. This combination is permanently fixed into my psyche. It is still my favourite meal of all time. When my brain is left to medical research, they will find an entire lobe dedicated to the pleasure experienced from this combination.

So, from the 1960s to the present day, the Koh-I-Noor brings those fond memories flooding back. I would have to say that after 50 years, the Koh-I-Noor was part of my coming of age, what I value in food and who I am. It is engrained into our culture. The Koh-I-Noor is as traditionally Scottish as Oor Wullie, fitba' and Irn-Bru. And, oh yes...I always did order an extra portion of pakora!'

—Gerard Graham
Author of Checking Out of the Hotel Euthanasia

'Arriving in Glasgow in 1965 as a 17 year old from the sedate cultural backwaters of Ayrshire, my sole experience of curry, like 98.5% of the Scottish population at that time, was confined to bits of cardboard chicken laid out on soggy rice and lightly covered in a bland spice-less sauce, all answering to the name of VESTA Curry.

The Koh-I-Noor Restaurant was not the first Indian Restaurant I visited in Glasgow, the Green Gate on the corner of Bank Street had that dubious honour, but a quick tour of all neighbourhood establishments soon identified a belief never relinquished, that The Koh-I-Noor was the best Indian restaurant in Gibson Street , and therefore the best in the western world.

Within a month of starting University I had settled into an almost universally shared student lifestyle involving somewhere between 3 and 6 curries a week, generally washed down before, during and after with copious quantities of beer.

Forget your Rangers or Celtic, your Labour or Tory, for my and many subsequent generations of Glasgow students, the defining binary identity choice was Koh-I-Noor devotee or Shish Majal supporter. I liked the food in the Shish Majal, and enjoyed tolerable curries in the Shalimar and the Green Gate, but the favoured place, the one for Birthday and special event curries, for weekly celebrations and for the best curry of the week, it was always the Koh-I-Noor for me.

The routine was always the same, a welcome at the door from Rasul, the always present "front of the house" presence. A big man of great charm and obvious charisma, he had a fantastic memory, always welcoming you by name and remarking on your last visit before ensuring you were ushered to an appropriate table. The first two course never changed, crisp poppadoms with delicately spiced onions, followed by perfect Pakora, usually vegetable. Then the key dilemma of every visit, was it to be luscious lamb or creative chicken?

The very first curry I ever had in the Koh-I-Noor, a truly Kennedy moment almost everybody seems to remember clearly, was chicken curry. A wonderfully satisfying dish that sealed my affection for both curry and Koh-I-Noor. Over the next months and years, I experimented with many more exotic sounding chicken dishes, from your madras and bhoona, through jaipuri, masala, kashmiri, karahi, and many more. But magnificent as they all were, time and again I would return to my first love. It would be a misleading insult to describe it as a plain chicken curry, full of delicacies and taste as it always was. In no other restaurant would I ever order "just a chicken curry" but it always and still remains my favourite Koh-I-Noor chicken dish. The current menu describes it as chicken curry (traditional style)—the perfect description.

My second Koh-I-Noor curry was a lamb bhoona, in the days before the Full Bhoona was perfected en route to becoming a key part of Glasgow language as well as culture. Again I instantly fell in love, with the rich thick sauce and the melting meat. And while over the years I have flirted with other lamb dishes, especially Rogan Josh and Lamb and Ladyfinger, in many other establishments, I have always maintained the Koh-I-Noor Full Bhoona as my favourite lamb dish.

After four years of this wonderful curry education I left for six years in the arid curry-free fiefdom of Fife where only the occasional trip to Glasgow reminded me of what I had lost. Returning forever to Glasgow in 1975, I resumed a lifestyle where curries played a crucial part. I broadened my range to include some Ashokas, Balbirs and Mother Indias and even Wee Curry Houses, but I never lost my love for the Koh-I-Noor and sustained it through their move to Charing Cross, their introduction of their breath-taking Buffet, and the transfer of responsibility from Rasul to the equally charming and charismatic Waseem.

Over the years I have seen many famous people dining in the Koh-I-Noor alongside me, from Billy McNeil to Donald Dewar and many more, but Rasul and Waseem have the welcome knack of making it clear to every punter, celebrity or not, that they are a special guest and equally welcome.'

—Sandy Jamieson
Author of three football books, three novels, and most recently A Subtle Sadness

'Both myself and Jim Dey have been going to the Koh-I-Noor since '64, I think—that's in the days when it was in Gibson Street and the food came up from the basement in a dumbwaiter. It was Waseem's grandfather who was doing the cooking at the time—I believe he was the first person to introduce pakora in Glasgow—he called them 'indescribables' at the start. If you wanted a carry-out back then you had to take a pot in for yourself—there weren't any containers.

Then Rasul, Waseem's dad, was owner, you always felt welcome in his restaurant. He was a great host, and a bit of a practical joker. Jim was the same way—we would go to the restaurant after the pubs had shut and Jim would do a neat wee trick—he used to get a chapati and slip it surreptitiously inside his shirt and then ostentatiously open his shirt up and scratch it—people thought his skin was falling off!'

—Walter Kerr
Loyal Customer

'Walter and I have been going to the Koh-I-Noor ever since the sixties. I sort of discovered the place by accident one night—I went in for a meal and absolutely loved it, then went back to a flat I shared with Walter and a couple of other guys and raved about it. So Walter came with me a couple of nights later and the rest is history!

My girlfriend and I got married in Martha Street and we asked Rasul if we could have our wedding reception in the Koh-I-Noor. I think it must have been the first wedding he's ever done and we had a great time with all of our friends. It was great having an Indian feast to celebrate. We were both students—my wife a nurse and myself an architect and all of our friends were West-enders mostly in the same boat.

As Walter said, we would order a few more chapatis than we needed and stuff some in our pockets. Then, when you got on the bus you'd put it on your chest under your shirt, open it up and start scratching. People were horrified at you because it looked like very unhealthy skin.

As I said, I was an architecture student at the time, and when Rasul found out he asked if I could draw up some plans for the restaurant to reflect what he was thinking in terms of making changes. Money never changed hands—he'd just feed me the odd curry or two! They were terrific days.

There weren't many Indian restaurants at the time but due to the quality of food and service, we've stayed loyal to the Koh-I-Noor ever since. He used to give us New Year calendars. One night, maybe 10 years ago after the restaurant had moved to Charing Cross, my wife and I were in having a curry and he said "we're closing the front door in a moment, there's a VIP coming but you can stay—we'll vouch for you." Big Range Rovers with tinted windows arrived and blocked off our car in fact! In came John Reid for a meal. He sat at one table alone for a curry, and at another table sat all of his bodyguards. Once we'd finished they moved their cars and let us away! The fact that the Secretary of Defence would stop in specifically to the Koh-I-Noor for a curry, showed us that—in our minds anyway—he had good taste.

A number of years ago, the *Sunday Times* reviewed the Koh-I-Noor and they said that the waiters' diamante studded waistcoats, which were wine red with gold trim and rhinestone studs, made them look like India's Hell's Angels!

The sauces are good and the food has never really changed and I think that's why a lot of people fell in love with it and keep their loyalty to the place. The lamb is always moist, filled with flavour and soaking up the sauce.

Back when Rasul asked me to help do the restaurant up, other Indian restaurants I worked on were going for designer, minimalistic, sleek interiors and, strangely enough, his father didn't want that at all. All he wanted was the feel of a traditional Indian eating house and the Koh-I-Noor was initially designed very simply in that manner. He wanted a circular fountain which I took and adapted into the walk-round for the buffet. Then, he wanted the side room tented with fabrics he brought back from Pakistan, the kind which would be used for a wedding celebration. He also brought back hand-painted chairs and pictures of rural life in Pakistan. Rather than trying to be designer and clever, he stuck to what he knew, and I think in many ways that's been to his credit because the restaurant has an authenticity about it. The curry has always been consistent and the place has never been pretentious.'

—Jim Dey
Loyal Customer

'My links with the Koh-I-Noor go back to 1981, however my mother first visited it in 1964, and now my children frequent and enjoy it, so my family has an unbroken 53-year, three generation relationship with the restaurant.

I think it essential to set the context in which the restaurant opening is set. Today there is no shortage of exotic food on tables in Glasgow and elsewhere. I was born in 1962, and can remember the 60s. The only fast food was fish and chips, and fish fingers caused a revolution. Italian food was available in a few places and was considered exotic. Apart from football shirts, I remember the 1960s as a monochrome decade. Then the Koh-I-Noor opened.

My uncle took my mum to the Koh-I-Noor soon after it opened. I can't imagine she had anything too spicy that time, but she was a regular visitor.

1980 saw me starting to study dentistry at the University of Glasgow. The preclinical studies for the first two years were at the Gilmorehill site in the west end. The last two weeks of first year were quite frantic, with exams, sometimes more than one, every day. The last exam was on Friday lunchtime, and after an Irn-Bru in the Glasgow University Union, my thoughts and those of my colleagues turned to food. One mate, Allan, was already a regular at the Koh-I-Noor. He suggested we have a takeaway, but this was uncharted territory for me. His recommendation was a lamb bhoona. I tried it, and was hooked. All the way through dental school, the Koh-I-Noor was our favoured Indian (although was and is run by a Pakistani family) restaurant. It may be worth mentioning that all the way through that time at university I worked as a waiter in a French restaurant in a hotel on the south side of Glasgow. The menu allowed only relatively few choices, and was in French. There was a dress code: no tie meant no entry. It was very staid. I enjoyed working there, and it financed my studies, but I was struck between the formality of that establishment and the hustle, hustle and informality of the Koh-I-Noor. It was even possible to buy a jug of Irn-Bru for the table in the latter establishment, and I have to say it took me a while to adapt to eating the nan breads and chapatis with my hands!

Now, I'd like to say that our relationship with the Koh-I-Noor was unbroken, however there was a hiatus. After a particularly heavy rainfall, the River Kelvin was swollen and in spate, and the aforementioned pillar collapsed rendering the extension unsupported, and demolition was mandated. After a gap of perhaps two years (I am unsure of the specifics) the Koh-I-Noor reopened in what had been the glamorous Berkeley function suite. This represented not just an increase in size, but an ambitious city centre location, sumptuous surroundings, and waiting staff with stunning embroidered waistcoats. My family and I continued to frequent the Koh-I-Noor until 1993 when I moved to England for a new job. Even so, for the last 23 years when I visit Glasgow and curry is on the menu, the Koh-I-Noor is the venue. I have taken colleagues for meals there, and continue to recommend it to anyone who requests suggestions for eateries in and advance of visiting the city. My children (aged 23, 20 and eight) have gone from being very young, and did not take long to migrate from chicken nuggets to more exotic fare. My son has travelled to Glasgow with work, and of course took his colleague there. There were 17 members of my immediate family, and for birthdays and at Christmas we met at the Koh-I-Noor over the years.

Favourite dishes? For me the pakora, vegetable or fish, for starters, and the spicy onions with the poppadoms are worth looking forward to. Even the chicken tikka masala is more spicy there than my son and older daughter get in Lancashire where we live, so it does have a wee kick. I like the buffet, and sometimes used to go for the tandoori chicken. As a student I was on a tour of France and Andorra by train. I got dreadfully sunburnt, and very hungry as my student savings did not go very far. First evening back in Glasgow, it was for a meal with my mum at the Koh-I-Noor, definitely chicken tandoori for me. The sweet naan is unlike any we have tried elsewhere, and my youngest daughter goes for it every single time. But for me, the original and best, is lamb bhoona. The meat is melt-in-the-mouth tender, it is spicy and fruity, and fabulous. I *never* have lamb bhoona anywhere else.

Recently my mother passed away. The family wanted to eat together that night. There was only one logical, friendly and appropriate place: the Koh I Noor.'

—Gary Cousin
Loyal Customer

The three generations of the Cousin family who have been dining at the Koh-I-Noor

'As I approached my 18th birthday my best friend and I were invited for a few beers in the Beer Bar at Glasgow University Students Union and an Indian curry by my friend's elder brother and his friend, both second year students. At this time, students existed on student grants—not loans. But, like students today, the grants never lasted long. Consequently, the enterprising pair that my newfound friends were would invite curry 'virgins' for beer then a kofta vindaloo on the premise that the newbies would be unable to handle such a hot dish and relinquish it to the ever-hungry older pair. This was the first time that I would enter the Koh-I-Noor but certainly not the last. I am proud to say that my friend and I survived the ordeal of this, the hottest curry available at the time, and indeed it became a favourite. A few years later and a student myself, my friends and I would twice-weekly partake of a curry—especially after having a couple of pints. That always seemed to be the trigger. About that time a letter from a research scientist appeared in the Glasgow *Herald* suggesting that the chemicals in the curry sauce released endomorphs into the brain—hence the apparent curry addiction. Soon, there were a number of curry houses in Gibson Street but only the Shish and the Koh-I-Noor ever maintained the regular clientele and even today only these two exist from that area, albeit relocated.

I always preferred the curries that Rasul would provide, especially the 'Full Bhoona' which has been described and explained how the term has entered Glasgow vernacular. We were offered other examples of the cuisine, but we all mostly stuck to the few old favourites the menu continues to offer. Sometimes, when awaiting a carry-out, Rasul would ask that I go to the Shish and get a particular meal from 'his cousin,' which he would examine—basically checking out the competition.

After discussing the matter with other restauranteurs on the street, alcohol began to be served in the restaurants. This meant an opportunity to take advantage of the better licensing hours. Sometimes my friends and I would find a piece of chapati in our pockets the next day and eventually remember that we got it to sustain us on the walk home as we had missed the last bus.

As we got older we still went to eat at Rasul's but long gone were the days when we could eat three curries a day. But then, lager was two shillings and three pence and a bhoona lamb madras was four and six!

Rasul would often comment that we (Glaswegians) ate hotter curries than they (his staff) ate! There is something about Glasgow curries that seem to separate them from those elsewhere in Scotland. Yes, I accept that the style and flavour of curry differs from the Punjabi style offered by Rasul. But I now live in Ayrshire and the curries are not the same—they are alright, but never as good as Glasgow curries overall. A trip a number of years ago found us surprisingly in a very small curry shop on the Isle of Millport. Commenting to my wife that this reminded me of a Koh-I-Noor meal led the waitress to bring from the kitchen her husband, who, it transpires, worked previously for Rasul.

Twenty years ago, for work reasons, I was in Birmingham, which resulted in a few beers and a curry with colleagues. As I left, I helped a couple struggling with a pram and two small children exit the restaurant. This resulted in a few friendly words being exchanged with the husband who said that it pleased him to hear my accent, commenting that he studied at Glasgow and indeed worked part-time as a waiter at a restaurant near the university. Of course, it was the Koh-I-Noor.

Although we have been going to and getting carry-outs from the Koh-I-Noor for many years (I am now 66) I have never seen anyone famous, despite the pictures of the great and the good that adorn the walls. However, almost everyone I know in Scotland has either been to or heard of the restaurant. What amazes me is the way that Rasul would always remember you and take the time to ask after you and your family. A skill that has been passed down to Wasseem. My brother and some work colleagues were taken to the restaurant by a senior member of the company up from down South to impress the troops. He wanted to take them to a restaurant he had been advised was the best and was confident that it was unknown to him. When all were seated he seemed impressed as Wasseem approached him with a broad smile. Less impressed when he was totally ignored in favour of my brother.

Both father and son have always been generous in giving advice on making curries but never revealing the marinade for their lamb. There were a few times also when they gave me and other friends milk and sugar to take home, before the shops seemed to be open all the time.

But what else keeps them going? Why are they such good a restaurant? The food, obviously, but what about location? In Gibson Street when we were students, excellent, but we have left uni and live elsewhere; the service, the staff in general, ambience? The price? A meal no longer costs what it did when we were students, but then, we get paid more.

My friends and I had many good times and meals there after a few beers and discussing how to put the worlds to right. We took girlfriends who became wives and then our children who now regularly enjoy their meals there with their children.

When I sit in the Koh-I-Noor, I find it hard to believe that for nearly 50 years Rasul and now Waseem have provided me with excellent food and a place to share good times with my friends.'

—George Ibell
Loyal customer

I first started eating at the Koh-I-Noor around 1985. As students, myself and between eight and 10 friends were regulars every Saturday at 12:30pm for a "curry breakfast." We reckoned it was the best cure in the world for our Friday night hangovers! Indeed, one of my friends claimed that he invented the lamb and mushroom curry one Saturday, when two of the group shared separate lamb and mushroom curries; creating the combo that you can order from the restaurant's menu today – I'm not so sure about this but it's a great story (or myth) that we've carried for over 30 years.

Over the years some of my friends have moved away for work, one even to the other side of the world in Australia, but the place they all want to return to when they come home is the famous Koh-I-Noor. Myself and two of the original group can still be found in the restaurant most Saturdays, though we've moved the curry breakfast time nearer to 4pm! In my mind, the Koh-I-Noor does the best nann bread in the world – it's absolutely outstanding. Waseem, the current member of the family to run the restaurant, is himself a great cook and his chicken tikka karahi is the best ever. The restaurant is also a place for a family celebration. My own family members love it and we regularly have birthday and Christmas celebrations in the restaurant. On one occasion I visited with my nephew and Billy Connolly was having a meal with Tom Ferrie - the Scottish radio presenter. My nephew got a little star struck but that lifted when, after witnessing how well I was being treated by Waseem and the front-of- house team, he proudly proclaimed "Brendan you are getting even better treatment than Billy Connolly!"

I'm blessed to be a customer of the Koh-i- Noor.

Brendan Murphy, Coatbridge
a very regular customer for 32 years.

My husband and his family have eaten in the Koh I Noor for many years. I remember my first visit. I was instantly drawn to the beautiful smells and sensational tastes and we've continued to eat here regularly as an extended family ever since, celebrating birthdays, Christmas, stag nights and many more family occasions. This picture reminds us of a night we ate in the restaurant and were greeted by a surprise diner - Mr Billy Connolly. We were desperate to speak to him but felt it inappropriate to intrude in his meal. Our little baby boy was dressed in a Santa suit and Billy and his company were drawn to his attire. Billy was very relaxed and approachable in the Koh I Noor as he agreed to pose for these pictures, much to our delight. We enjoy the relaxed atmosphere and the staff are very attentive and helpful. The food is second to none - especially the Rogni Nan which we could eat for starter, main and desert!! We look forward to many more family nights in the Koh I Noor with Waseem and the team.

Laura and Richard Devine

The Devine Family with Billy Connolly

76

Photos from the Dining Room

Billy Connolly has been a regular visitor to the Koh-I-Noor, from when it first opened to the present day.

1960s

1970s

1980s

As the photos show, the hair, the clothes and the face have changed over the years but Billy's love for and devotion to the Koh-I-Noor has never wavered.

1990s

2000s

2010s

Rasul and Lulu in the 70s

Waseem and David Anderson

Waseem with the Right Honourable
Lord John Reid, Baron of Cardowan

Waseem with the Capercaillie folk band

Derren Brown and Waseem

Peter Powers and Waseem

Recipes

Waseem and Rasul adding some new dishes to the menu

Recipes from the Kitchen

The food is, naturally, at the heart of the Koh-I-Noor, growing from those traditional family recipes Waseem's grandmother served when they first opened their doors, to the menu you see today. In the following pages are some of the Koh-I-Noor's best loved recipes, written by the chefs for you to recreate at home.

Although some of the recipes and ingredients may seem simple, the methods are true. The philosophy of the food at the Koh-I-Noor has always been about traditional, homecooked curries that capture the simple, classic flavours of a curry. These recipes are straight out of the restaurant kitchen, in their purest form, and have been presented here with simple ingredients and instructions for an authentic taste.

Rasul enjoying another field trip to Pakistan this time with the family

Breads

Starters

Sides

Vegetarian

Chicken

Lamb

Sweets & Drinks

Breads

For gluten-free chapati (above), use gram flour instead of whole wheat flour

Chapati

Serves 4

Chapati, also known as roti, is an unleavened flatbread from the Indian Subcontinent, popular in India, Nepal, Sri Lanka and Pakistan. Made from whole wheat flour, it is cooked on a flat skillet, or 'tava' and is ideal served with dips and curry.

Method

1. Place the flour in a large mixing bowl along with the salt.
2. Add the water, a little at a time, and mix until you have a soft dough.
3. Tip the dough onto a lightly floured surface and knead until it's firm yet elastic.
4. Divide the mixture into four balls, flatten each ball slightly, then roll out to a flat disc, dusting with flour as necessary.
5. Heat a griddle or shallow frying pan. Lay the chapati on the griddle or pan and cook for about 20 to 30 seconds or until the surface is bubbling.
6. Turn the chapati over and cook on the other side for a further 10 to15 seconds. As soon as brown spots appear on the underside, it's done!
7. Repeat with the other chapatis and serve fresh.

Ingredients

125 g of whole wheat flour, plus extra for dusting
A pinch of salt
1 tbsp of oil
60 ml of water

Paratha

Walter Kerr's favourite bread at the Koh-I-Noor!

Parathas are a flat bread that originated in the Indian subcontinent, and are prevalent throughout India, Pakistan and Burma. This recipe is a simple, plain paratha, but these flatbreads can be stuffed with lamb mince or vegetables and made a meal in themselves.

Method

1. Mix together butter, flour, oil, and salt in a bowl. Add water, a little at a time, and mix to form a tight dough.
2. Knead well until you have a soft, pliable dough. Rest for 30 minutes.
3. Divide the dough into 8 pieces and roll into balls.
4. On a lightly floured surface, roll out one ball into a large, thin rectangle. Keep the other balls covered with a damp cloth.
5. Brush the rolled-out dough with a little ghee, then fold ⅓ of the dough inwards, brushing with ghee, then fold the bottom end up over it, as if you are folding a letter, and brush again with ghee.
6. Repeat this folding method again until you have a square shape, brushing with ghee in between steps.
7. Roll the square out so you have an even, square paratha, then fry in a pan over a medium-high heat until brown spots appear. The dough will bubble and puff up as the layers separate.
8. Repeat with the other dough balls, keeping the others warm in a low oven while you cook them.
9. Serve warm with dips and curry.

Ingredients

1 tbsp butter
200g all-purpose flour
1 tsp oil
1 tsp salt
Water, as required
2 tbsp ghee

Naan Bread

You can't beat this classic flatbread! This recipe keeps things simple, with no need to add yeast or knead for an extensive period of time. Key to their success is a super-hot grill!

Method

1. For the dough, sift the flour and salt in a bowl.
2. In another bowl, mix together the milk and oil.
3. Make a well in the centre of the flour mixture and pour in the milk mixture, then slowly mix the dough by working from the centre and incorporating the flour from the edges of the well to make a smooth, soft dough.
4. Kneed well for 8 to 10 minutes, adding a little flour if it gets too sticky.
5. Place the dough in an oiled bowl, cover with a damp tea-towel and leave in a warm place for up to an hour, then form the dough into 5 balls.
6. Preheat the grill to high and place a heavy baking sheet on the upper shelf of the grill.
7. Roll each of the dough balls out into a thin teardrop shape.
8. Sprinkle over your chosen topping and press into the surface of the dough.
9. Place the naans onto a hot baking sheet and grill for just 1 to 2 minutes, or until slightly browned, then brush with butter and serve hot.

Ingredients

800 g of self-raising flour
1 tsp of salt
100 ml of milk
1 tbsp of oil
Nigella or poppy seeds, to serve (optional)
1 tbsp of melted butter, to serve

Starters

Mince Samosa

Serves 6

Samosas are a fried, or sometimes baked, snack generally filled with a savoury filling of minced lamb or beef, cheese, peas or lentils. Its size and shape vary, although it is most commonly recognised in its triangular form. This version is filled with lamb mince and peas, and baked for a lighter snack.

Method

1. Preheat the oven to 200C/180C fan.
2. Heat 1 tbsp of the oil in a large frying pan over a medium heat. Add the onion, ginger and garlic and cook until just golden brown.
3. Add the cumin, chilli powder and salt. Cook for a further minute.
4. Add the mince and cook for 10 to 15 minutes until brown. Add the peas and cook for a couple more minutes.
5. To assemble the samosa, take 4 sheets of filo pastry and cut it into thirds lengthways. Brush lightly with oil.
6. Place a spoonful of the mince filling at the top of each strip, then fold over and over to form triangular parcels. Place on a baking tray.
7. Repeat this process with the rest of the mixture and the filo – you should end up with around 9 samosas.
8. Place the baking tray filled with the samosas in the preheated oven and bake for 30 to 35 minutes until golden and crisp, turning halfway through the cooking time.
9. Serve hot garnished with fresh coriander.

Ingredients

1 tbsp of oil,
plus extra for brushing
500 g of lamb or beef mince
2 cloves of garlic
1 tsp of cumin
1 tsp of fresh root ginger
1tsp of red chilli powder
1 tsp of salt
½ cup of peas
Fresh coriander for garnish
12 sheets of filo pastry

Onion Bhaji

Serves 4

Not dissimilar to the pakora, the onion bhaji is, again, one of the most popular Indian starters or snacks. Usually served as a topping to Indian meals, it's now more commonly served as a starter or side dish. Filled with delicious, fragrant onions, these portable snacks are full of flavour.

Method

1. Sieve the flour into a large mixing bowl, then add the spices and stir to distribute them evenly.

2. In a separate bowl, beat the eggs, then add the sliced onion and stir to coat.

3. Add the egg-coated onion into the flour mixture, stir to coat well, and leave to stand for ten minutes.

4. Heat the oil in a large, heavy-based saucepan over a medium-high heat.

5. Fry the mixture in small batches, then drain on kitchen paper and serve hot.

Ingredients

4 large onions, roughly sliced
2 free range eggs
150 g of plain flour
1 tsp of cumin
1 tsp of chilli powder
1 tbsp of fenugreek
Salt to taste
Cooking oil, for frying

Paneer Chilli

Serves 2 to 3

This vegetarian dish is full of spice and heat, and can be served as a starter, side or even roll them into chapatis for a tasty and spicy wrap! This recipe is a dry one so don't worry if you don't have much of a sauce to go with it.

Method

1. Marinade the tofu in the chilli powder, cornstarch, pepper and salt and set aside.

2. Heat 1 tbsp of the oil over a medium heat and fry the paneer cubes until golden brown on all sides, then place on a plate and set aside.

3. In the same pan, heat the remaining oil and cook the onion, peppers and chilli until beginning to soften, then add the chilli and tomato sauce and stir to combine.

4. Tip the paneer back into the pan, stir to coat in the sauce and serve hot, garnished with fresh coriander and more green chilli, if you like.

Ingredients

300 g of paneer, cubed
1 tbsp of cornstarch
¼ tsp of red chilli powder
¼ tsp of crushed black pepper
¼ tsp of salt
2 tbsp of oil
1 small onion, diced
1 green pepper, chopped
3 to 4 green chillies, sliced vertically (seeds removed if you don't want it too hot)
1 tbsp of chilli sauce
2 tbsp of tomato sauce

Vegetable Pakora

'Favourite dishes? For me the pakora, vegetable or fish, for starters, and the spicy onions with the poppadoms are worth looking forward to.'
—Gary Cousin

Serves 4

This traditional fried snack, derived from the Sanskrit, pakvavata, translates as 'a cooked small lump', or its derivative, vataka, 'a round cake made of pulse fried in ghee', is one of the most popular side dishes in Indian and Punjab cuisine. Today, it comes in many forms, from chicken, to the increasingly popular fish version. This recipe goes back to the classic vegetable version.

Method

1. To begin with, prepare the vegetables by shredding the spinach and finely slicing the onion.

2. Grate or very finely chop the potatoes – this is important to ensure they cook with the other vegetables.

3. Put the vegetables in a large mixing bowl, then add the spices and sieve in the flour, stirring to coat everything evenly.

4. Add the water, a little at a time, until you have a thick batter that coats the vegetables.

5. Heat the oil on a medium-high heat in a large, heavy-based saucepan.

6. Once the oil is hot, use a large spoon to take small portions of the batter mix, and fry until golden brown and crisp.

7. Drain on paper towels and serve hot with raita and pakora sauce.

Ingredients

450 g of plain flour
Water, as required
1 tsp of chilli powder
1 tbsp of coriander seed
1 tsp of cumin seed
300 g each of onion, potato, and spinach
Cooking oil for frying
Salt, to taste

Sides

Boiled Rice

Serves 4

An everyday staple in most kitchens, this recipe will help you get the best boiled rice to serve alongside our delicious curry recipes.

Method

1. Place the rice, salt and oil in a large, heavy based sauce pan.
2. Add the water to the pan, then place over a medium high heat and bring to the boil.
3. Change the heat to low, cover with a tight-fitting lid and leave to cook for 10-15 minutes.
4. Remove the lid, give the rice a stir, drain if necessary and serve hot.

Ingredients

800 g of rice
4 litres of water
A pinch of salt
1 tbsp of oil

Pilau Rice

Serves 2

The classic accompaniment for any Indian meal, pilau rice is flavoured with cumin and turmeric to give it that classic yellow glow. Feel free to add toasted almond flakes, peas or sultanas to spice up this rice dish.

Method

1. Preheat the oven to 150C/120C fan.

2. In a large pan with a tight-fitting lid, put the rice, water, oil and spices over a medium heat and cook until all the water has been absorbed, stirring regularly to ensure it doesn't stick.

3. Once the water has been absorbed, stir the rice to ensure it is evenly cooked and coated in the spices, then place in the oven for 10 minutes to fluff up.

4. Serve hot with curry of your choice.

Ingredients

800 g of basmati rice
2 tbsp of sunflower or vegetable oil
1 tbsp of salt
1 tbsp of cumin
1 tsp of turmeric
1.5 liters of water

Pakora Sauce

This tomato-based sauce is the perfect pairing for fried pakora, be it chicken or vegetable. As with the spiced onions, this recipe keeps things simple and lets the ingredients shine through.

Method

1. Finely chop the onion and mix with the red chilli, tomato sauce, mint sauce, and tamarind, then season to taste. The dip should be pinkish-red in colour.
2. Serve immediately with mixed pakora, or store in the fridge for a couple of days until needed.

Ingredients

1 large onion
1 tsp of salt
1 red chilli, finely chopped, seeds removed
2 tbsp of tomato sauce
2 tbsp of tamarind paste
1 tbsp of mint sauce

Raita

This is one of many dips and sauces traditionally served at an Indian feast. This cooling dip is a great contrast to the bright, spicy flavours of curries, or to dip your pakora and bhajis into! As mentioned, the recipes here are based on simple ingredients true to the original Indian and Punjabi recipes, so don't try to over-complicate the dips. You can, if you wish, add some fresh mint leaves however.

Method

1. Place the grated cucumber on a piece of kitchen paper, gather up the edges, and squeeze to remove the excess moisture.
2. Place the yoghurt in a bowl and add the cumin, cucumber, and onion, stirring well so everything is evenly coated.
3. Season with salt and pepper and serve immediately with bread, curry, or sides of your choice.

Ingredients

500 g of natural yoghurt
½ a cucumber, grated
½ of an onion, diced
1 tbsp of cumin
Salt & pepper to taste

Spiced Onions

Generally accompanied by crisp poppadoms, the Koh-I-Noor recipe for Spiced Onions keeps things simple, with just three ingredients, making them easy to whip up in just a couple of minutes.

Method

1. Finely slice the onion and place in a mixing bowl with the chilli, tomato sauce and some salt for seasoning.
2. Stir to ensure everything is well combined and serve with poppadum or chapatis with mango chutney or raita for an array of different flavour options.

Ingredients

1 onion
1 tsp of chilli powder
2 tbsp of tomato sauce
Salt and pepper, to taste

Vegetarian

Dal Chana

Serves 2

Chana dal is also known as Bengal gram, and the lentils have a sweet, nutty taste to them. They come from black chickpeas and are split and the outer cover is removed. This recipe is heavily spiced with classic flavours and is great as a side dish or served with flatbreads. You can now buy chana dal from most supermarkets in the world food aisle.

Method

1. Heat a saucepan over a medium-high heat and add the oil, followed by the onion, ginger, chilli and garlic and cook until turning golden brown.
2. Add the chilli powder, turmeric, cumin and garam masala to the pan and cook for a further minute.
3. Add the chana dal to the pan along with 200ml of water, stirring to ensure everything is well combined.
4. Cook over a medium heat until the dal is soft and the water has mixed with the spices to form a fragrant gravy.
5. Serve hot and garnish with fresh coriander.

Ingredients

300 g of dal chana
2 tbsp of oil
1 onion, diced
1 tbsp of fresh root ginger
1 tbsp of fresh garlic
2 green chillies, sliced, seeds removed
1 tbsp of fresh coriander
1 tsp of red chilli powder
1 tsp of turmeric
1 tsp of cumin
1tsp of garam masala

Paneer Karahi

Serves 2 to 3

Paneer is really versatile and a great meat substitute, but it's also a delicious ingredient that is used widely across north India. This dish is almost like an Indian stir fry, using fresh tomatoes and the zingy fragrance of coriander to create a full and flavoursome masala.

Method

1. Heat 2 tbsp oil in a pan over a medium heat and add the onion, garlic and ginger and fry until softened.
2. Add the tomatoes, a pinch of salt, and the spices, then increase the heat and leave to bubble gently.
3. Once cooked down, it should be a thick red sauce – add a splash of water if it is catching.
4. Add the red pepper and cook for a further 2 minutes.
5. In a separate pan, heat 1 tbsp oil and gently fry the paneer until browned on all sides, then add it to the sauce, stirring until the paneer is well coated.
6. Scatter with the spring onion and serve with chopped fresh coriander.

Ingredients

600 g of paneer, cubed
1 onion, diced
3 tomatoes, chopped
1 tbsp of fresh ginger, finely chopped
2 garlic cloves, crushed
1 cinnamon stick
1 tsp of ground coriander
2 tsp of chilli powder
1 red pepper, chopped
2 spring onions, chopped
Oil, for cooking
½ bunch of fresh coriander

Saag Aloo

Billy Connolly's favourite dish at the Koh-I-Noor!

Serves 4

A classic and well-known dish, Saag Aloo is the perfect accompaniment to your Indian feast. Full of spinach, potato, and spices, this is also a hearty vegetarian option.

Method

1. Heat the oil in a large non-stick frying pan on a medium heat, then add the onion and cook until beginning to soften.
2. Add the tomatoes and spices and cook for a further five minutes, then blend using a stick blender to make a thick tomato gravy.
3. Add the potatoes to the gravy and cook over a medium heat until softened, about 15 to 20 minutes, then add the spinach and cook for another five minutes.
4. When ready, the potatoes should be soft and tinged yellow from the spiced gravy, and the spinach should be wilted.
5. Serve hot topped with fresh coriander.

Ingredients

800 g of spinach
500 g of potato, cubed
2 onions, chopped
250 g of tomatoes, chopped
1 red chilli
2 tsp of turmeric
½ tsp of cumin seeds
½ tsp of ground coriander
1 tsp of fenugreek
2 of tbsp oil

Vegetable Bhoona

Serves 4

Probably one of the most popular curries in the UK, this bhoona is packed full of vegetables, but can easily be substituted for your favourite protein if you'd rather not go vegetarian. This is a slightly drier dish made with onion, garlic, and tomatoes.

Method

1. Heat the oil in a large pan over a medium heat and cook the onion, ginger, and garlic until beginning to soften.

2. Add the tomatoes and spices and cook over a low heat until the tomatoes have broken down and created a thick gravy, adding a little water to loosen it if necessary.

3. Add the potatoes, cauliflower, and carrots, stirring to coat the vegetables evenly, and leave to simmer until the vegetables are tender, then add the frozen peas.

4. Once the peas are cooked, take off the heat and serve hot with fresh coriander, or fresh green chilli for an optional kick!

Ingredients

200 g of potato, cubed
1 head of cauliflower, broken into florets
200 g of fresh peas
200 g of carrots, diced
2 onions, chopped
6 tomatoes, roughly chopped
2 tbsp of fresh ginger, finely diced
2 garlic cloves, crushed
2 tsp of chilli powder
2 tsp of turmeric
A pinch of fenugreek
4 tbsp of sunflower oil, for cooking

Chicken

Chicken Ceylonese Korma

Serves 4 to 6

Korma is the go-to dish for anyone who can't stand the heat. This Ceylonese version is cooked with cooling coconut cream for a fragrant, mild curry that doesn't skimp on flavour. As you can see, there is chilli included in the recipe, however this is optional if you want to keep heat out completely.

Method

1. Heat the oil in a large, deep frying pan over a medium heat and cook the onion, garlic, and chilli until soft and golden brown.

2. Add the spices and cardamom seeds and cook for a further two minutes.

3. Add the chicken and fry, stirring regularly, for ten minutes or until browned all over.

4. Add the cream and coconut cream, season to taste, and cook on a low heat for 15 to 20 minutes, or until the chicken is cooked through and the sauce has thickened.

5. The curry should be a lovely pale yellow colour, and is perfect served with pilau rice and naan.

Ingredients

4 large chicken breasts, cubed
250 g of onion, roughly chopped
1 red chilli,
de-seeded and chopped (optional)
2 cloves of garlic, chopped
2 tsp of turmeric
2 tsp of cumin
8 cardamom pods,
pods crushed and seeds removed
4 tbsp of vegetable oil
4 tbsp of single cream
4 tbsp of coconut cream
Salt, to taste

Chicken Chasni

Serves 4 to 6

This fragrant curry is flavoured with mango chutney and fresh mint, and finished with double cream. Rich but full of fresh flavours, this curry is sure to be a big hit with the sweet and sour clientele.

Method

1. Heat the oil in a large, deep pan over a medium heat, then add the onions and fry until soft and golden brown.
2. Add the garlic, ginger, and dry spices and cook for a further minute, then add the chicken breast and fry for ten minutes until golden brown, adding a touch of water or oil if it's beginning to stick.
3. Stir in the tomatoes, mango chutney and fresh mint and simmer on a low heat, stirring occasionally, for ten minutes, or until the chicken is cooked through.
4. Gradually stir in the cream and continue to cook for a further two minutes, then serve hot with rice or naan.

Ingredients

4 large chicken breasts, cubed
200 g of onion, roughly chopped
200 g of tomatoes, chopped
4 cloves of garlic, crushed
½ tsp of fresh ginger, chopped
1 tbsp of salt
1 tbsp of chilli powder
1 tbsp of turmeric
2 tbsp of mango chutney
1 tbsp of fresh mint, chopped
2 tbsp of single cream
2 tbsp of oil, for frying

Chicken Curry

'It would be a misleading insult to describe as plain, full of delicacies and taste as it always is. In no other restaurant would I ever order "just a chicken curry" but it always has been and still remains my favourite dish.'
—Sandy Jamieson

Serves 4 to 6

Not buried under specific names or titles, this classic chicken curry is one of the more simple and traditional dishes on the Koh-I-Noor menu. A recipe passed down for generations, it is still one of the most popular dishes in the restaurant.

Method

1. In a large, deep pan, heat 2 tbsp. of oil over a medium heat then add the cloves, cardamom pods and cinnamon stick.
2. Stir the spices around and allow them to release their fragrances for about five minutes.
3. Add the remaining oil along with the onion, tomatoes, garlic, and ginger, and cook until soft and golden.
4. Carefully remove the cloves, cardamom and cinnamon from the pan. This will stop anyone biting into them later.
5. Add the remaining spices, along with the chicken, and mix well to combine, then cook over a low heat for 10 minutes, stirring regularly to stop anything sticking to the bottom of the pan.
6. Add enough hot water to the pan to just cover all the ingredients and bring to the boil, then reduce the heat back to low and let it cook for 25 to 30 minutes, or until the chicken is cooked through, stirring occasionally, until you have a thick, dark brown gravy and tender meat.
7. Serve hot with rice and naan bread.

Ingredients

4 large chicken breasts, cut into bite size chunks
250 g of onion, chopped
200 g of tomatoes, chopped
3 cloves of garlic, crushed
30 g of fresh ginger, chopped
8 whole cloves
8 whole cardamom pods
200 ml of vegetable oil
1 cinnamon stick
½ tsp of fresh coriander
½ tsp of cumin
2 tsp of chilli powder
1 tsp of turmeric
Salt, to taste

Chicken Lyallpuri

Serves 4 to 6

The Koh-I-Noor's take on Madras, made with fresh ingredients such as coriander and green chillies to give a nice kick to the dish. This Chicken Lyallpuri is a dry curry, so don't be put off by the lack of wet ingredients. This curry is fragrant with spice and due to the lack of gravy, can catch at the bottom of the pan, so keep an eye on it. Serve it with dips like raita and fresh flatbreads.

Method

1. Heat the oil in a large, deep frying pan, over a medium heat, then add the onion and fry for ten minutes until soft and turning golden brown.

2. Add the spices and chilli and cook for a further two minutes until they begin to colour and the spices release their fragrance.

3. Add the chicken to the pan and brown on all sides.

4. Add the tomato puree and continue to cook over a medium-low heat until the chicken is cooked through, adding a touch of water or oil if the mixture is beginning to stick.

5. Serve hot with lots of dips and flatbreads.

Ingredients

4 large chicken breasts, cubed
300 g of onion, roughly chopped
2 tsp of chilli powder
1 tsp of turmeric
1 tsp of cumin
2 green chillies, de-seeded and chopped
1 tsp of paprika
1 tbsp of tomato puree
4 tbsp of vegetable oil
Salt, to taste
½ bunch of coriander to flavour

Chicken Tikka

'My favourite dishes at the Koh-I-Noor? Well, it's hard to look past the properly-marinated chicken tikka. Mmm…think I'll pop round for one right now.'

—Tam Cowan

Serves 2 to 3

Originating in the Punjab region, chicken tikka is traditionally made using small pieces of boneless chicken marinated in yoghurt and spices. This recipe uses succulent chicken breast and traditional flavours to create a delicious, authentic starter.

Method

1. Preheat the grill to its highest setting.
2. Combine all the ingredients above, minus the chicken, in a large mixing bowl until you have a smooth, orange-yellow marinade.
3. Add the chicken to the marinade and leave for a minimum of two hours – can be made the day before and left to marinade overnight.
4. Thread the marinated chicken pieces onto skewers and place onto a grill tray.
5. Grill for ten minutes, turning regularly, until cooked through and serve hot with raita and flatbreads.

Ingredients

450 g of chicken breast, chopped into chunks
100 ml of lemon juice
1 tbsp of salt
2 tsp of chilli powder
4 cloves of garlic, crushed
1 tbsp of fresh ginger, grated
½ tsp of cumin
4 tbsp of yoghurt
2 tbsp of oil

Lamb

Lamb Bhoona

'I have a traditional taste. In general my favourite meat at the Koh-I-Noor is Lamb Bhoona'
—Mian Sadiq

Serves 2

The dish that the Koh-I-Noor is famous for, this lamb bhoona recipe is filled with all the classic flavours and is ideal served with pilau rice, flatbreads or a big salad for a bit of freshness.

Method

1. Heat the oil in a large frying pan (a wok works well) over a medium heat.

2. Add the cumin seeds and stir until beginning to colour and releasing their fragrance, then add the onion, ginger and garlic and fry for five minutes until turning golden brown.

3. Add the fenugreek, chilli powder, coriander and turmeric, followed by the tomato, and cook for a further five minutes until the tomato begins to collapse.

4. Add the meat, cook for five more minutes, then add 125ml of water and bring to a simmer.

5. Continue to cook the curry until the lamb is tender, then serve hot garnished with fresh coriander.

Ingredients

400 g of lamb
1 tsp of cumin seed
2 tsp of coriander
1 tsp of fenugreek
1 tbsp of fresh ginger
1 tsp of fresh garlic
1 large onion
1 medium tomato, chopped
1 tsp of red chilli powder
1 tsp of turmeric
Salt, to taste
1 tsp of chopped green coriander
3 tbsp of oil

Lamb Biryani

Serves 2 to 3

Biryani is an Indian meat and rice dish, all rolled into one. Making biryani can be time-consuming, but the results are worth it. This recipe adds tender chunks of lamb, perfect for slow cooking.

Method

1. Heat the oil in a large non-stick saucepan over a medium heat, then add the onion and garlic and fry until beginning to soften.
2. Add the spices and cook for a further 2 minutes until beginning to release their fragrances.
3. Add the lamb and brown on all sides.
4. Tip in the rice, stir to combine, then pour in the water until everything is covered.
5. Turn the heat down low, and leave to cook for about 20-30 minutes, checking regularly.
6. After 30 minutes, the water should be absorbed and the rice cooked. Give everything a good stir to ensure everything is mixed and well combined, then serve hot!

Ingredients

500 g of basmati rice
500 g of diced lamb
1 onion, diced
2 garlic cloves, crushed
1 tbsp of salt
1 tsp of cumin
1 tbsp of chilli powder
1 tsp of garam masala
4 tbsp of sunflower oil
1 tbsp of fresh coriander
About 2 litres of water, as required

Lamb Garam Masala

'I like a lamb curry with plain rice on a couple of chapatis and ice cream as a nice finish to the curry.'
—Jim Dey

Serves 2

Lamb is a popular meat in Indian and Punjabi cuisine as it is cheap to buy and great for slow cooking. This recipe is a semi-dry curry and is flavoured with turmeric, cumin seeds, and garam masala.

Method

1. Heat a large frying pan over a medium head and add 1 tbsp of oil.
2. Add the onion with the ginger and garlic paste and cook until turning golden brown, then add the spices, tomatoes and remaining oil and cook for 5-10 minutes to make a thick gravy.
3. Add the lamb and simmer over a gentle heat until the meat is tender, about 1 hour.
4. Serve hot garnished with fresh coriander and green chillies.

Ingredients

500 g of lamb
75 g of ginger garlic paste
1 onion, chopped
½ tsp of turmeric
½ tsp of cumin seed
½ tsp of red chilli powder
½ tsp of garam masala
75 g of tomatoes, chopped
80 ml of oil
Salt, to taste
Fresh coriander and green chilli, for garnish

Lamb Seekh Kebab

Serves 4 to 6

Cooked simply under a grill or on a barbecue, these spicy lamb kebabs are easy to make and full of flavour. For ease when moulding the meat onto the skewers, keep your hands wet to avoid the mixture sticking, and even run cold water over the outside of the kebab occasionally to help create a smoother finish.

Method

1. Preheat the grill to its highest setting.
2. In a large bowl, mix the mince with the all the ingredients until well combined, then place the mixture in the fridge for an hour to firm up and allow the flavours to develop.
3. Take the mince out of the fridge and divide the mixture into 6-8 balls.
4. With wet hands, slowly spread the mince mixture onto skewers until you have a hot-dog shaped kebab, making sure the kebabs are quite thick.
5. To help shape the kebabs, keep your hands wet to avoid the mixture sticking.
6. Place the kebabs under the grill and cook for 10 minutes, turning regularly, until cooked through and golden brown.
7. Serve hot with fresh coriander and a variety of sauces and salads.

Ingredients

400 g of lamb mince
50 g of fresh coriander, chopped
100 g of onion, finely chopped
100 g of fresh ginger, finely chopped
3 garlic cloves, finely chopped
2 green chillies, de-seeded and chopped
1 tsp of chilli powder
1 tsp of salt, plus extra to taste
½ tsp of cumin seeds
½ tsp of ground coriander
½ bunch of fresh coriander for garnish

Sweets & Drinks

152

Fruit Chatt

An Indian version of the classic fruit salad, the fruit chatt is spiced with chatt masala powder and garnished with fresh mint for an aromatic twist. The chatt masala powder typically consists of cumin, coriander, ginger and chilli, and can now be found in the world food section of most supermarkets. Choose your favourite fruits to make this recipe your own.

Method

1. Wash and dice all the fruit and place in a large bowl.
2. Mix in the sugar, lemon juice and chatt masala, and stir so everything is well coated.
3. Garnish with some fresh mint and serve cool.

Ingredients

1 banana
1 small bunch of grapes
1 mango
1 guava
1 apple
1 orange
1 tsp of lemon juice
Chatt masala powder, to taste
1 tsp of sugar
A handful of fresh mint, to garnish

Indian Masala Tea

Serves 1

A simplified method of making this spiced tea, this recipe brings the flavours and aromas of India into your teacup. Classic flavours of cinnamon, clove and cardamom are infused into the water to create an aromatic experience. Serve with as much or as little milk and sugar as you like.

Method

1. Heat the water in a small saucepan over a medium heat.
2. Add the tea bag, followed by the cinnamon stick, cardamom pods, and clove.
3. Bring the water to the boil, allowing the tea and spices to be released into the water.
4. Remove the teabag and spices, serve piping hot and add milk and sugar to taste.

Ingredients

250 ml of milk
2 tbsp of water
1 tea bag
1 cinnamon stick
4 cardamom pods, crushed
1 clove
2 tsp of sugar

Kheer

Serves 6

Not entirely different to a British rice pudding, this dish, originating in India, is flavoured with cardamom and pistachios, and slow cooked to ensure the rice is super soft and light.

Method

1. Put the rice and milk in a large saucepan over a very gentle heat.
2. Cook the rice for about three hours until the rice is soft and the milk has been absorbed.
3. Add the cream, sugar, ground almonds, half the pistachios, and the cardamom pods, and stir to combine.
4. On a very low heat, continue to stir the rice to distribute the pistachio and cardamom and heat the cream. The rice should be soft, sweet and creamy.
5. Garnish with the remaining pistachios and serve warm.

Ingredients

1kg of rice
2 litres of milk
1 tbsp of sugar
4 green cardamom pods, crushed to release seeds
4 tbsp of single cream
100 g of ground almonds
100 g of pistachios, ground

Sweet Lassi

Serves 2

The same yoghurt based drink that Waseem's grandfather drank on the fields in Pakistan, this cooling, sweet drink will keep you full for hours with the high protein content, but also hit those sweet cravings. You can top this drink with any variety of chopped fruit or nuts, in this recipe, we've added pistachios.

Method

1. Put the yoghurt into a large mixing bowl, then add the chilled milk and sugar.

2. Ideally using a wired whisk, churn it thoroughly for at least 5 minutes until the sugar dissolves.

3. Add half of the pistachios and churn again to create a frothy layer.

4. Pour the drink into glasses filled with ice cubes, top with the pistachios and serve chilled.

Ingredients

400 g of natural yoghurt
3 tbsp of sugar
150 ml of milk, chilled
2 tbsp of crushed pistachios
A handful of ice cubes, to serve

The search for the next recipe continues

On a field trip to Pakistan

On a field trip to India

Glossary

If you are new to cooking Indian and Punjabi cuisines, some of the words, spices and ingredients can be confusing. This glossary contains the phrases and ingredients you will encounter regularly, and should help to give a better understanding of the items used.

Spices and Ingredients

Cardamom: The pods are frequently used in Indian cooking to flavour rice and sweet dishes. The pods are lightly bashed in a pestle and mortar generally, which helps release the seeds. Cardamom has a strong, unique taste, with an intensely aromatic, resinous fragrance. The green cardamom pods can be expensive, but you don't need very many to impart their flavour.

Chatt Masala: Used to make fruit chatt, chatt masala is a spice powder mix used in Indian and Punjabi cuisine. It typically consists of amchoor (dried mango powder), cumin, coriander, dried ginger, salt, black pepper, asafoetida (hing) and chili powder. It is becoming more widely known in the UK and, as with ghee, is beginning to appear in supermarket world food aisles.

Cloves: May be used to give aromatic and flavour qualities to hot beverages, often combined with other ingredients such as lemon and sugar. They are a common element in spice blends such as pumpkin pie spice and speculoos spices. It pairs well with cinnamon, allspice, vanilla, red wine and basil, as well as onion, citrus peel, star anise, or peppercorns.

Coriander: A very popular spice in Indian cuisine, coriander comes in three different forms: seed, ground or fresh. Ground coriander seed loses flavour quickly in storage and is best ground fresh. Coriander seed is a spice in garam masala and Indian curries which often employ the ground fruits in generous amounts together with cumin, while fresh coriander is commonly used as a final garnish.

Cumin: Also known as zeera, cumin is a very popular spice and is present in most curry recipes. It comes in both seed and ground form and helps to add an earthy and warming feeling to food, making it a staple in certain stews and soups, as well as spiced gravies such as curry and chilli.

Garam Masala: The composition of garam masala differs regionally, with many recipes across India according to regional and personal taste, and none is considered more authentic than others. The components of the mix are toasted, then ground together. A typical garam masala contains peppercorns, cloves, cinnamon, nutmeg, cardamom, bay leaf, cumin and coriander.

Ghee: Used regularly in Indian and Punjabi cuisine, ghee is a class of clarified butter, originating from the Indian subcontinent. It is prepared by simmering butter, skimming impurities from the surface, then pouring and retaining the clear, still liquid fat and discarding the solid residue left over. It can now be easily found in most large supermarkets in the world food aisle.

Methi: Better known in English as Fenugreek. It is an annual plant in the family Fabaceae, with leaves consisting of three small obovate to oblong leaflets. It is cultivated worldwide as a semiarid crop. It is used in almost every Indian preparation be it dal, paratha or curry.

Paneer: A common meat substitute in Indian cooking, paneer is an unaged, acid-set, non-melting cheese ideal for cooking in curries or grilling in kebab form. Paneer is the most common type of cheese used in traditional Indian and Pakistani cuisines. It is sometimes wrapped in dough and deep-fried or served with either spinach or peas.

Paprika: A ground spice made from air-dried red bell peppers, sometimes with the addition of chilli peppers or cayenne peppers. Paprika is used as an ingredient in numerous dishes throughout the world. It is principally used to season and colour rice, stews, and soups, and its smoked variety adds a subtle smoky flavour to dishes.

Tamarind Paste: Made from the ripened flesh of this fruit, which is sweet and has a distinct flavour. It is often used in desserts, as a jam, blended into juices or sweetened drinks, and can be a key ingredient in flavouring curries and rice. If you can't find any, lime juice mixed with an equal quantity of light brown sugar can work as a substitute.

Turmeric: A member of the ginger family, turmeric is widely known for its health benefits and potent yellow colour. Turmeric is one of the key ingredients in many savoury Asian dishes, imparting a mustard-like, earthy aroma and pungent, slightly bitter flavour to foods. It is ideal for adding yellow colour to pilau rice and flavour to curries.

Breads

Chapati: Also known as roti, is an unleavened flatbread from the Indian Subcontinent, popular in India, Nepal, Sri Lanka and Pakistan. Made from whole wheat flour, it is cooked on a flat skillet, or 'tava' and is ideal served with dips and curry.

Naan: A leavened, oven-baked flatbread found in the cuisines of West Asian, Central Asia and South Asia. Naan is traditionally cooked in a tandoor, from which tandoori cooking takes its name. This distinguishes it from roti, which is usually cooked on a flat or slightly concave iron griddle called a tava.

Paratha: A flatbread that originated in the Indian subcontinent, Paratha is an amalgamation of the words parat and atta which literally means layers of cooked dough. Some parathas can also be stuffed with minced meat or vegetables.

Author's Acknowledgements

It's not every day you are approached to write a book, so when Ringwood asked me to write the story of the Koh-I-Noor, I was both honoured and thrilled. This project has been a yearlong labour of love and determination from three different corners, and I'm proud of what we have achieved.

I firstly want to thank Waseem Tahir and the Koh-I-Noor team for putting their faith in me and their story in my hands. It was such a delight to hear Waseem retell stories from his childhood, and tell me about his incredible family, who created the Koh-I-Noor legacy. To hear what an impact this long-standing restaurant has had on Glasgow food culture is fascinating for a foodie like myself, and it was an honour to learn about the Tahir family and the hard work they have put in over the last fifty years. I must also thank the customers who have contributed to this book, sharing their stories and their love of the restaurant and of the Tahir family.

I am indebted to the Ringwood team, particularly Sandy Jamieson and Harley Griffiths, who not only gave me this opportunity, but continued to support and reassure me every step of the way. Thank you for your guidance, hard work and patience. No book is the work of one individual, it is a team effort that requires a range of skills, and I'm lucky to have had a thoughtful and professional team working with me.

Finally, thank you to my husband, Sam, and my family, for listening to my ideas, for sharing their own, and for supporting me through this entire process.

—Amy Glasgow